NERO

Leaders of the Ancient World

NERO

Zoe Lowery and
Julian Morgan

ROSEN
PUBLISHING
New York

Published in 2017 by The Rosen Publishing Group, Inc.
29 East 21st Street, New York, NY 10010

First Edition

Library of Congress Cataloging-in-Publication Data

Names: Lowery, Zoe, author. | Morgan, Julian, 1958– author.
Title: Nero / Zoe Lowery and Julian Morgan.
Description: First edition. | New York, NY : The Rosen Publishing Group, Inc., 2017. | Series: Leaders of the ancient world | Includes bibliographical references and index. | Audience: Grades 7–12.
Identifiers: LCCN 2016021383 | ISBN 9781508172567 (library bound)
Subjects: LCSH: Nero, Emperor of Rome, 37-68—Juvenile literature. | Emperors—Rome—Biography—Juvenile literature. | Rome—History—Nero, 54-68—Juvenile literature.
Classification: LCC DG285 .L69 2017 | DDC 937/.07092 [B] —dc23
LC record available at https://lccn.loc.gov/2016021383

Manufactured in China

CONTENTS

INTRODUCTION

Information about Nero's life stems from two kinds of primary sources. The first type is the written evidence from Dio Cassius in books 61 to 63 CE of his *Roman History*, Tacitus in the *Annals of Imperial Rome*, and imperial biographer Suetonius. Secondly, there is also a wealth of archaeological evidence found in the city of Rome itself, including the Golden House that Nero built, as well as in other outposts of the empire. Also important are inscriptions on public buildings throughout the empire, as well as coinage, which provides valuable portraiture and other information.

Nero's impressive archaeological remains more or less speak for themselves, but we get the majority of our information about his life from a mere trio of Roman historians, all of whom portray the infamous emperor as wicked to the core. Beginning with Tacitus's version, history has portrayed the emperor as heartless. And because these three authors incorporated at least some amount of exaggeration into their accounts, it's a tricky trail trying to decipher fact from fiction. Regardless, Nero's character, his legacy to the modern world,

Nero has been vilified in many accounts, but there may be more to his story than can be found in the three traditionally consulted historical accounts.

is forever tainted by the view of these authors. Two of the three were not even alive at the same time of Nero and Tacitus was but a boy.

Nero's later depictions in Christian literature did little to improve his reputation with comparisons to the Antichrist. From there his character moved to the sensationalized, with portrayals as a foolish, a spineless murderer, and a leader who fiddles as Rome burns. In short, he was eventually simplified into being no more than a monster.

But was he? Archaeological journalist Marisa Ranieri Panetta helps provide a little context in her conversations with *National Geographic*'s Robert Draper: "But look at the great Christian emperor Constantine. He had his first son, his second wife, and his father-in-law all murdered. One can't be a saint and the other a devil. Look at Augustus, who destroyed a ruling class with his blacklists. Rome ran in rivers of blood, but Augustus was able to launch effective propaganda for everything he did. He understood the media. And so Augustus was great, they say. Not to suggest that Nero was himself a great emperor—but that he was better than they said he was, and no worse than those who came before and after him." It's worthwhile to note that the now-infamous story of Nero fiddling merry music as Rome burned was written more than a century later.

To say the accounts of his character remain mixed is an understatement. Tacitus records that Nero insisted that there be shelter available for the homeless. He motivated the industrious to help rebuild the city by offering to pay them. Besides putting fire safety codes in place, he made sure those rules were followed. He built gymnasiums and other phenomenal Roman structures, too. It's unlikely that historians will ever agree on how to frame the life of a man who also brutally persecuted Christians. But of course, there is far more to the Emperor Nero than a fiendish, foolish fiddler. Keep reading to delve into the life of a memorable emperor.

CHAPTER 1

A RULER IS BORN

Nero was born on December 15, 37 CE, to Cnaeus Domitius Ahenobarbus and Agrippina. Nero was only three years old when his father died and the emperor Caligula banished his mother, Agrippina, for her involvement in a conspiracy against him. So Nero's early childhood was spent with his aunt.

MOTHER AND SON

His mother was allowed back into Rome after Caligula's death, when Claudius became emperor in 41 CE, and she eventually became the new emperor's fourth wife. It was Agrippina's evil character that shaped Nero and determined many of the events of history to follow, including his rise to power. Agrippina was notoriously lax in her

FAMILY TIES

When future emperor Nero was born on December 15, 37 CE, his father, Cnaeus Domitius Ahenobarbus, said that any child of his would have a detestable nature and would become a public danger. This prophetic remark was not a good start for the boy, whose full name at birth was Lucius Domitius Ahenobarbus. His family had a reputation for cruelty, arrogance, and extravagance, which had passed down through the generations to this child. Nero's grandfather had been famous for his skill as a charioteer and had been decorated after a military campaign in Germany, though he was also known as a vicious individual. Nero's father was said to have killed a freedman of his for refusing to drink as much as he was told, to have gouged out the eye of a nobleman in the Forum, and to have deliberately run over and killed a boy on the Appian Way.

morals, using her beauty as a weapon to secure wealth and fame. She managed and manipulated her new husband Claudius so that Britannicus, his son from a former marriage, was sidelined in favor of his new stepson, Nero. Agrippina also arranged the murder of Domitia Lepida, the aunt who had looked after Nero during her time away from Rome in exile. This may have been because Domitia was Britannicus's grandmother, and would be likely to support his cause.

PRINCE OF THE YOUTH

Nero was made consul designate at a very early age, soon after putting on his toga of manhood in 51 CE. This meant that the highest political office in Rome had been reserved for him, though he would not hold the post for another four years. In the meantime he was called the prince of the youth. Rather ironically, he was also designated the protector of Britannicus, on the suggestion of the emperor's freedman Pallas. A marriage to Claudius's daughter Octavia was arranged for him by his mother in 53 CE to strengthen Nero's closeness to the emperor. This came about even though Octavia had already been betrothed to another man, the hapless Lucius Junius Silanus Torquatus, who was accused of incest with his sister and thrown out of the Senate, according to the historian Tacitus.

Although Nero was made consul designate at an early age, several years would pass before he would actually take the position.

According to records, Agrippina might have had her own husband Claudius, murdered to ensure her son's success.

However, Agrippina worried more and more that her own boy, Nero, might be hampered in his path to power by his stepbrother Britannicus as he grew older, so she met with the known poisoner Locusta. She arranged to murder her husband Claudius by giving him poisoned mushrooms to eat, before he could take steps to help move his own son's career forward. In the wake of Claudius's death, on October 13, 54 CE, Nero was proclaimed emperor by the praetorian guards, the handpicked bodyguard of the imperial family, who took him to the Senate where the fathers of the city accepted him. Nero was sixteen years old and had just become ruler of the mightiest empire in the world.

From the age of ten, Nero had been taught by one of the leading literary figures of his day, Lucius Annaeus Seneca, who now stayed with the young emperor as his advisor. Seneca had originally come from Cordoba in Spain and was a remarkably wealthy and powerful man. He was well known as an orator, writer, and a Stoic philosopher, though he had been exiled some years before to Corsica for having an adulterous affair with Claudius's niece, Julia Livilla. It was thanks to the influence of Agrippina that he had been restored to Rome, some time after she married Claudius. Seneca was assisted by Sextus Afranius Burrus, the prefect of the guard who had engineered Nero's proclamation as emperor, and by Nero's mother, who stayed as close as she could to the center of power. While Seneca provided the intelligence and academic stimulus, Burrus was a calm and controlled individual who originally came from Vaison la Romaine in the south of France and had a very real strength of character. Both men were extremely wealthy, having financial interests and influence spreading far across the Roman Empire. For some time, it appeared that the young emperor and his trio of helpers would rule Rome well, and he seemed to heed the advice he was given. People overlooked the rumors of Claudius's murder, and when Nero spoke about him publicly he did so with respect. Claudius was made a god, and a temple to him was built on the Caelian Hill in Rome.

A REIGN OF CLEMENCY

It was important that Nero's image be kept as clean as possible at the outset of his reign, and Seneca urged him to make "clemency" his watchword.

Clemency meant that Nero would be understanding and forgiving, an emperor of the people who would try his best to emulate Augustus, the first emperor of Rome. Whereas Claudius had been very obviously influenced, and to some extent controlled, by his personal staff of freedmen, Nero said that he would listen to advisers and restore some power to the Senate. He wanted to put an end to trials carried out in the emperor's personal rooms, separating the imperial house from the process of law and government more than had been the case under his predecessor. He tried to appear forgiving and to create an image for himself of kindness. He once said, "How I wish I had never learned to write!" when asked to sign an execution order. The Senate placed restrictions on lawyers, preventing them from taking fees or bribes. At the same time, Nero relaxed the need for junior magistrates to put on gladiatorial shows, which was expensive and therefore restricted some men from being able to hold official posts. Also, Nero rejected the Senate's offers to call him "Father of the Country" and to change the beginning of the year to December, when he had been born.

Furthermore, Nero made it unnecessary for

This coin shows both Nero and his mother Agrippa. Agrippa was a strong influence on her son's rule during his younger years,

consuls to swear an oath to support the emperor rather than the state, making it seem that he had a genuinely positive attitude to shared government. He allowed Plautius Lateranus to return to Rome from exile. Lateranus had been thrown out by Claudius for having an affair with his third wife, Messallina. It seemed that Nero would be a considerate and careful emperor by listening to the advice of the Senate, acknowledging its advice, and even refusing its offer of a perpetual consulship. Coins from the time bear an acknowledgment of the Senate's approval of their issue, which is a tangible sign of his respect. This was a good start, though a good number of problems would have to be solved soon.

Agrippina became Nero's co-ruler, which was not mandated by law but was recognized in a variety of other ways. Nero is said to have used the password "the best of mothers" with his palace guards, and early coins of the reign show both Nero's and Agrippina's heads facing each other. Although she was not allowed to attend Senate meetings, a door was built to the rear of the Senate house so she could listen in on the debates. On one occasion, Nero was sitting on a platform waiting to receive a delegation of Armenians. As they approached, his mother seemed to try to move next to him. Seneca told the young man to stand and advance to meet the embassy, thus avoiding a breach of protocol. At that time a woman would not have been allowed to stand on the imperial dais next to the emperor without compromising his authority.

FAMILY CONFLICT

It seems, however, that mother and son often did not see eye to eye, and quarrels soon arose between them. Her affair with the freedman Pallas, who had been a senior executive and financial secretary on Claudius's staff, led to real disagreement, resulting in the dismissal of Pallas from the imperial household in 55 CE. At this time Agrippina thought she was losing influence with her son and considered promoting the interests of her stepson Britannicus, who in many ways would have been a natural heir to the throne of his father Claudius, with a better claim to power than Nero had.

Nero quickly became well aware of the challenge before him as Britannicus neared his fourteenth birthday and prepared to wear a toga. But

Agrippina's stepson, Britannicus, became a challenge to Nero, who, perhaps following in his mother's footsteps, had his stepbrother poisoned.

before Britannicus would officially become a man, he ate a poisoned dinner, thanks to Nero. When asked about his stepbrother's death, Nero argued that Britannicus had a seizure. With the murder of his blameless brother, Nero's real personality came through; he was cruel and insensitive. His actions were an eerie echo of his own' mother's decision to free up the throne by killing Claudius.

CHAPTER 2

BRIGHT BEGINNINGS?

The initial five years of Nero's reign have been described as some of Rome's best times by the emperor Trajan. At the same time, however, there was a lot going on in the background. Efforts to influence the young emperor by Burrus, Seneca, and Agrippina created an atmosphere of secrecy in the palace. Meanwhile, Nero was involved in several love affairs, including one with a freedwoman named Acte, and his mother Agrippina did not approve of his actions at all.

In these early years Nero seems to have kept some very unhealthy company, parading through the streets of Rome late at night, causing mayhem and havoc wherever he went. The historian Tacitus says that Rome came to resemble a conquered city at times. Sometimes the riotous behavior caused real problems, as when Senator Julius Montanus

AGRIPPINA LOSES HER GRIP

One of the emperor's good friends, Marcus Salvius Otho (who later became emperor himself for a short time), had a very attractive wife named Poppaea who was keen to advance herself by any means possible. Otho was eventually sent away to be governor of the Spanish province of Lusitania so that Nero and Poppaea could carry on an affair in his absence. This caused great annoyance to Agrippina, who urged Nero to stick with his wife Octavia. Nero had little love for Claudius's daughter, however, and the rift between mother and son grew.

Gradually Agrippina lost her influence with Nero, and her image no longer appeared opposite his on coins. Agrippina's imperial guards were taken away from her, and she was removed from Nero's palace in Rome. It was reported that she wanted to marry Rubellius Plautus, the grandson of the emperor Tiberius, and that she would then try to rule without Nero.

Nero's ambitious lover Poppaea seemed like a source of trouble to Agrippina, but Nero would not be swayed.

was involved in a brawl with Nero. Later on, the senator sent a letter apologizing to the emperor for hitting him, but he was then forced to commit suicide for this action.

In the meantime there were more rumors. One was that Seneca and Burrus were plotting to replace Nero with Claudius's grandson, Faustus Cornelius Sulla Felix, who was eventually sent off in exile to Massilia, modern-day Marseilles, in France.

POPULAR EMPEROR

Nero seems to have been advised well for much of this time; his personal popularity in Rome was considerable. How far he formulated his own policy and how far he was ruled by the philosopher and the guard prefect we cannot ascertain, but many measures taken at the time kept his people happy. In particular, Nero attempted to keep the grain supply secure, completing improvements to the harbor in Ostia. He also ensured that grain ships were not counted as taxable property, thus making them a good business investment. Twice, a donation of 400 sesterces was made to each citizen of Rome. On another occasion, 40 million sesterces were paid into the public treasury to maintain public credit levels. Nero attempted to reduce the number of taxes levied on goods traded, though in this he was not entirely successful. He did abolish a 4 percent tax on slaves. Tax claims going back more than one year were abandoned and soldiers were exempted from paying any tax at all except on what they sold.

Nero helped many retired soldiers settle into homes and improved the political status of some towns as part of this drive. Pompeii and Tegeanum became Roman coloniae, which meant that their citizens had full Roman citizenship, which at that time was not normal throughout the Italian peninsula. In 57 CE Nero built a new amphitheater for public entertainments in the Campus Martius area of Rome, declaring, however, that nobody should be allowed to die there for the sake of entertainment. He also declared that senators should fight in the arena, which was not at all a popular suggestion with them. Nero held the office of consul in 55, 57, 58, and 60 CE. He showed his respect for the Senate on a good many occasions. Once, after a riot in the amphitheater in Pompeii in 59 CE, he

A riot in Pompeii's amphitheater in 59 CE, illustrated here, caused the gladiatorial games to be canceled for a full decade.

referred the case for judgment to the Senate, which then banned the Pompeians from holding any more gladiatorial games for ten years.

MURDER!

Five years after becoming emperor, in 59 CE, Nero had become so resentful of his mother that he resolved to have her killed. There are different stories about their relationship, and they may even have been lovers. But it seems that it was particularly due to Agrippina's dislike of Poppaea that Nero made his decision. He may also have been influenced by his lover's resentment, as Poppaea made fun of him, calling him a mother's boy. He called his advisers together and consulted with them about how to murder Agrippina, relying heavily on his ex-tutor, a freed-

Nero tried to have his mother murdered by constructing a ship that would collapse on her, as illustrated here in *The Shipwreck of Agrippina* by Gustav Wertheimer.

man called Anicetus. The decision was made to invite Agrippina to dinner at Baiae near Naples, on the coast of Italy, and then take her home in a ship that would be so constructed as to collapse and sink during the voyage. When the leadweighted canopy over her head fell down, however, Agrippina was saved by the arms of her couch, which stuck out and prevented her from being crushed by the debris. Her maid Acerronia called out for help, saying that she was Agrippina and in need of help, but she was killed by a blow to the head from an oar. This was a warning to her mistress that it was a real murder attempt, not an accident. She then swam to shore and managed to return to her villa in safety, though in some considerable distress now about what might happen to her next. Nero then received a message from Agerinus, a freedman of Agrippina, who came to him to announce her "fortunate" survival. A knife was planted on the unlucky Agerinus, who was accused of coming to murder the emperor on his mistress's orders.

Nero then sent Anicetus to Agrippina's house at night to murder her. She had been deserted by all her slaves and was found by her assassins when they burst into her chamber. She urged her killer to strike her in her womb, where Nero had been born. It is said that the emperor went to see the corpse of his mother and admired her physical beauty as she lay dead before him. Nero now became terrified of public outcry. He spread the rumor that Agrippina had tried to kill him and declared her birthday a day of ill-omen. He wrote to the Senate, saying she had been killed after Agerinus's attempt on his life. She had interfered in government and her death was an act of providence.

AN END TO GOOD TIMES

After the murder of Agrippina, Nero's so-called five good years came to an end. It seems that while his mother was alive she may have caused him to use restraint, which when combined with the influence of Seneca and Burrus, had held him in check. His popularity with the upper classes of Rome began to suffer, as they regarded his actions as insulting and demeaning to them.

Nero's nastier nature appears to have reared its ugly head after his mother's murder. Instead of acting like a respectable emperor, he began ruling like an oppressive ruler. His Subiaco villa was

When his plan to have his mother killed in an alleged shipwreck failed, Nero had her murdered. Nero even went to see her body, as illustrated by Antonio Rizzi.

struck by lightning in Subiaco in 60 CE. Soon rumors spread that the strike was a sign that Nero would be replaced as ruler. To make sure that did not happen, Nero evicted someone who might have a claim to his throne: Tiberius's descendant Asia Rubellius Plautus.

CHAPTER 3

IN THE PUBLIC EYE: SPORTS AND OTHER SPECTACLES

Sometime around 59 CE, Nero formed a group called the Augustans. This was a collection of upper-class young men who worked as a kind of personal, private bodyguard group. Besides protection, the men would join him in public performances of gymnastics or other artistic acts.

SHOCKING SHOWMAN

Nero was a very keen showman who had a passion to take part in all kinds of activities. He had a private circus, or racetrack, built for him in the Vatican valley where he competed as a singer and charioteer before his selected public. It is hard to understand today how much impact this would have had then. The performing arts were seen as degrading, something to be done by Greeks for

Shown here are the remains of the theater at Nicopolis, where Nero may have performed as a singer or as a charioteer.

Roman entertainment. In wanting to sing, recite, and compete, Nero was behaving in a rather un-Roman way.

The members of the Senate and other nobles who were compelled to witness such activities must have felt very uncomfortable. It is interesting to note that ordinary Roman citizens, or plebeians, probably enjoyed the shows and the chance to see their emperor perform in person, but this was never reflected in the reaction of the upper classes.

Nero, however, was undeterred. It seems that his enthusiasm knew no restraint, and he hurled himself into his performances with increasing determination. He raced chariots around his circus and celebrated his *lud juvenales*, or young men's games, where he shaved off his beard in public. He had voice training

Nero's enthusiastic performances at his circus may have shocked the Senate and other nobles while entertaining most other Roman people.

and even embarked on strange diets to improve the quality of his singing, lying down with sheets of lead on his chest to improve his diaphragm. Historians believe that he refrained from eating apples, as they may have been bad for his voice.

NERO'S GAMES

In 60 CE Nero instituted the first so-called Neronia, or Nero's Games, where he staged events including athletics, chariot racing, musical contests, poetry recitals, and even oratories. The games were to be held every fifth year and were held again in 65 CE, but were discontinued thereafter. This was an attempt to have an event in Rome along the lines of the Olympic Games. Nero himself competed as a harpist and also won a prize for oratory. Many of the Augustans also competed, as did others, including professional athletes.

In 61 CE, Nero built a gymnasium in Rome and encouraged senators and other nobles to attend. He even offered them free oil with which to anoint themselves. Nero also built a complex of baths in the city. He carried on with his literary efforts, completing a poem called the *Sack of Troy*,

Nero made improvements to the Theater of Marcellus, or Teatro Marcello, which was originally constructed by Julius Caesar.

which was to get him into trouble in later times. It has been suggested that Nero may have had some real ability as a writer, perhaps more so than as a singer, since despite all his training and dieting he apparently had a thin and rather reedy voice.

Nero's suspicion of the upper-class Romans around him grew as their hostility to his hobbies made them withdraw from him. The death of the guard prefect Burrus in 62 CE may have been due to natural causes, though there were some suggestions that Nero had him poisoned for some unknown reason. Seneca asked to retire, but Nero would not allow him to do so, saying he still needed his advice and help. The emperor appointed two successors to the post of guard prefect, Faenius Rufus and Gaius Ofonius Tigellinus, the latter a low-born Sicilian who had previously suffered banishment from Italy for his crimes. Tigellinus had a marked effect on Nero and seems to have been a terrible influence on him.

One of Tigellinus's early achievements was to persuade Nero to have Rubellius Plautus killed in Asia where he was in exile, along with Faustus Cornelius Sulla Felix, who was in exile in Massilia. Plautus's head was brought to Nero, who is said to have exclaimed aloud to himself, "Nero, how could you have been so frightened of such a long-nosed man?" Sulla's head was brought to him, too, which Nero mocked for its gray hair.

The Senate reacted to this by congratulating Nero on his escape from the treachery of Plautus and Sulla, which may have only served to feed the emperor's growing self-deception. It seemed that

Nero could do no wrong, but if he did, the Senate would not only forgive him but even give praise. Two nobles, Antistius Sosianus and Fabricius Veiento, were tried for treason and banished, which seems relatively lucky for them, when compared with the fate of so many others. Sosianus had been accused of reciting improper satirical verses about the emperor at a dinner party. Nero had wanted a worse punishment than banishment for him, but the Senate's decision was a lenient one. Veiento was found guilty of using improper influence with Nero and of insulting senators and priests.

DIVORCING OCTAVIA

As a sign of his growing independence, Nero decided in 62 CE that his marriage to Octavia should be brought to an end. In a shameful deal that he struck with his freedman Anicetus, Octavia was accused of committing adultery with Anicetus and banished to the island of Pandateria, where she was later killed, her veins cut open as she lay in a hot bath. Her head was brought to Nero's mistress, Poppaea, the historian Tacitus tells us. Anicetus himself was allowed to retire to the island of Sar-

Nero depicted on a coin that was likely in circulation about 56–57 CE. Around 62 CE he divorced his wife Octavia, who is shown on the other side.

dinia as a reward for his lies, while Nero was free to marry Poppaea. Later in the same year she gave birth to a daughter, Claudia, who died about four months later. Poppaea took the name Augusta.

Throughout the next year, 63 CE, audiences at the theater at Neapolis, located in what is now known as Naples, enjoyed performances by a confident Nero. Previously, he had limited these appearances to private groups, some of which he selected himself, but Nero wanted to perform publicly and was no longer hesitant to about it. According to Tacitus, Nero wanted to appear in Naples because its origins were as a Greek city. Here, he believed audiences would appreciate his

Nero performed at the Neapolis theater, which is located in modern-day Naples. Here he began to perform more boldly than ever before.

art, and later he would spend four years touring a fantastical performance. First, however, Rome called for his attention.

CHAPTER 4

MEGALOMANIAC

For all his on-stage confidence, Nero could not shake his fear of anyone who might challenge his claim to the throne. This uncertainty also made him unsure as to how far he could push his absolute ruler title before he might create a complete government disaster. In 63 CE, for example, some of his informers blamed the great-great-grandson of Augustus, Decimus Junius Silanus Torquatus, of scheming against him. Nero's response was to force him to commit suicide.

From here, Nero's personal conduct only progressed from bad to worse. For example, he held a fake wedding, a so-called marriage to a young man called Pythagoras. It was in 64 CE, however, that things got particularly out of hand, and the scale of Nero's excessive ambition was seen for the first time by everyone around him.

ROME IN FLAMES

On July 18, 64 CE, fire broke out in Rome, starting in the Circus Maximus and spreading eventually to ten of the fourteen districts of the city. The devastation of Rome was on a scale never previously known and for nine days the fire raged wildly. Some of Rome's most historic buildings were destroyed forever, including the famous Temple of Jupiter built by Romulus and the Temple of Vesta.

Nero—who at the time was staying in Antium, where he was born—returned to Rome. He apparently took the lead in fire-fighting activities. Nonetheless, stories got out that instead he had been involved in a dramatic production, performing his poem about the sack of Troy in the Tower of Maecenas, overlooking the destruction. The story says that Nero "fiddled while Rome burned," referring to his ability as a kithara player. But should we believe this account? Probably not, though we cannot know for sure. He certainly did take steps to alleviate the suffering of his people by opening public buildings and his own gardens to the homeless. He also lowered the price of grain and helped to secure extra deliveries to the city from the port of Ostia.

Rumors flew that Nero watched and performed as Rome burned, but in reality he was not even in the city when the fire occurred.

REBUILDING ROME

However, it was during the aftermath of the fire that Nero laid himself open to personal attacks. He set about rebuilding the city with a positive attitude, laying down special regulations about new buildings so that each would have a colonnade at the front. Height restrictions were imposed as well. Builders were rewarded for keeping to their contracts or finishing their projects early, and many of the new constructions had to be carried out in stone, not wood. Nero even saw to it that the grain ships took the debris out of Rome when returning to Ostia. This was all seen as positive, but Nero earned much criticism when he undertook the biggest and most expensive building project ever seen in Rome, that of his famous Golden House.

The Golden House, or domus aurea, was a huge new palace, built to replace the previous, so-called domus transitoria, or corridor palace, which had connected the Palatine and Caelian Hills. The plan was to build not just between these hills, but also to extend the complex across onto the Esquiline Hill. The Golden House surpassed the earlier construction to an unbelievable degree. By using the

Nero built the Golden House, or *domus aurea*, to fill the void created by Rome's terrible fire. It was surrounded by extensive lawns and woods.

wasteland created by the fire, Nero created a huge park with lakes, lawns, and woodlands. The great house was faced with gold leaf and surrounded by a colonnade up to a mile in length, if we can believe the sources. It was in fact never finished, but inside it had elegant halls, beautiful high ceilings, and at its heart an octagonal chamber that may have had a revolving ceiling, allowing the diners to be showered with flower petals. The joint architects of the house were Severus and Celer, who also had a hand in much of the rest of Rome's reshaping. One popular rhyme described how the house was growing so big that it was threatening to reach the town of Veii, about 10 miles (about 16 kilometers) away:

> Rome's becoming a house.
> Romans, escape to Veii town,
> Unless the house
> Grows there too.

Nero himself said, "Good! Now at last I can live like a human being!" He had a statue of himself sculpted by Xenodorus, standing 120 feet (almost 37 meters) high, a constant reminder to his people of what he had succeeded in achieving at their expense. This great monument was called the Colossus, and later it gave its name to the Colosseum, the amphitheater built on the site during the time of the emperor Vespasian, when much of the Golden House was physically obliterated. It was buried under a mound of earth dug out to form the foundations for the new people's stadium. The Golden House itself was not rediscovered until the Renaissance period, when artists such as Michelangelo and Raphael were lowered into it on ropes so they could study the classical art found there and then model their own styles upon it. Today the Golden House is still open to visitors in Rome, a fantastic and vivid reminder of one man's megalomania.

SUSPICIONS

It was the scale of the building project that made people think that Nero must have started the fire deliberately, for they reasoned that he had profited greatly from his people's grief. The ongoing Golden House project was a visible reminder of his greed and arrogance, so resentment began to build up among the plebeians, the ordinary people of Rome. Nero chose to deflect the blame for the fire and said it was the Christians who had started it. Christians were publicly executed, thrown to the beasts in the amphitheater for popular entertainment, and even burned alive, having first been doused in oil and used as torches lighting up Nero's gardens by night. In the rash of persecutions that followed, Jesus's disciples, Peter and Paul, were put to death. However, this also worked against Nero, as popular opinion now came out in sympathy for the Eastern religious sect so brutally abused and tormented in this fashion. It should be made clear that this persecution was entirely political in nature. It did not spring from religious motives, as was the case in later times. The scale of spending on the Golden House took its toll on the economy, and Nero resorted to various measures to raise money to pay for it. Six landowners in northern Africa (part of the Roman Empire) were put to death so Nero could claim their estates and the revenue from them. Measures were adopted throughout the empire to raise money, and at about this time the weight of the coinage was altered so that a gold piece, which had previously weighed one-fortieth of one pound, weighed one-forty-fifth. Nero had another plan that was seen as crazy: to connect Lake Avernus, near Naples, to the river Tiber by means of a canal, thus connecting the port of Puteoli with that of Ostia, a distance of well over 100 miles (160 kilometers). This plan was shelved, presumably in view of the expense involved and the lack of funds available to pay for it.

PISO'S PLOT

By the start of the next year, 65 CE, Nero's popularity among the Roman nobility was at an all-

Nero decided to blame the fire on the Christians and had them killed in public, burned alive, or even thrown to the animals as a rapt audience watched!

time low. A conspiracy arose against him involving Romans from all walks of life, including senators, nobles, and plebeians. The details of the plot are unclear. It is called the Pisonian conspiracy, after Gaius Calpurnius Piso, believed to be the leader. Piso was a man of personal charisma who was loyal to his friends and generous. Historians believe his plan was to become emperor himself after killing Nero at games held in the Circus Maximus.

The plot was foiled because a woman named Epicharis gave information to Rear Admiral Proculus, who then notified the emperor. A series of interrogations followed, where friends and accomplices revealed each other to Nero and Tigellinus. The second guard prefect, Faenius Rufus, was an interrogator until he too was given away as a conspirator. Nineteen prominent men were killed after the plot's discovery, including the poet Lucan and Seneca, Nero's longtime adviser. The historian Tacitus remarks rather cynically that "after murdering his mother and brother, it only remained for Nero to kill his teacher and tutor." Others who lost their lives included Claudius Senecio, a close friend of Nero, and Plautius Lateranus. Piso committed suicide by cutting his veins. One of Nero's guard officers, Subrius Flavus, gave his reasons for involvement in the plot to the emperor as he was led off for execution: "I hated and detested you. I was as loyal as any soldier as long as you deserved my support. I began to hate you when you killed your father, when you murdered your mother, and destroyed your wife, when you became an actor, charioteer, and an arsonist." Nero was shocked to hear this. Normally, nobody ever dared to tell him what they honestly thought of him face to face.

Nero rewarded the imperial guard for their loyalty by giving them 2,000 sesterces each in addition to free grain. He summoned a meeting of the Senate and awarded honorary triumphs to Publius Petronius Turpilianus, Marcus Cocceius Nerva (who would become emperor in 96 CE), and Tigellinus, his guard prefect. Such triumphal honors were normally given to those who succeeded in major military campaigns, but this time Nero awarded them for saving him in the face of great danger and thus serving the state. Tigellinus's authority was extended; he was given increased control of the guard, which became a kind of secret police force. The month of April was renamed Neroneus, in the emperor's honor.

As a result of the Pisonian conspiracy, nineteen men were killed, including Nero's adviser, Seneca, as depicted in the painting, *The Death of Seneca* by Manuel Dominguez.

MORE VICTIMS

In the same year, 65 CE, Nero heard a story that Caesellius Bassus from northern Africa had seen a cave filled with the legendary Carthaginian queen Dido's treasure. With great enthusiasm, the emperor sent off a ship to gather up the collection of gold. He was enraged when he found out that the story was baseless.

Later that year, Nero's wife Poppaea nagged him for returning late from the games, and in a fury he kicked her to death. She was pregnant at the time, so this was doubly horrific. She was given a full state funeral, and her embalmed body was buried in the Mausoleum of Augustus. Some time afterward, Nero found a boy called Sporus, whom he had castrated and then married in a mock wedding ceremony because the boy reminded him of Poppaea. At another time, we are told, he also married his freedman, called Doryphorus.

After Poppaea's death, Nero took as his third wife Statilia Messallina, after putting to death her fourth husband, the consul Julius Vestinus Atticus. It seems that Nero's concept of marriage was as bizarre as many of his other ideas about life.

The second festival of the Neronia was held and Nero again performed in public, acting the parts of both men and women in a variety of roles. It is said that members of the audience often felt bored by his different performances but were compelled to sit through them. Suetonius tells us that some women pretended to give birth, while men feigned death, so they could be carried out of the shows. Others jumped off the rear wall of the theater just to escape, as the main gates were kept barred. The future emperor Vespasian was in the audience and almost fell asleep during one of Nero's performances. In view of this, Vespasian was lucky to be spared, as the emperor's enemies were by then often either killed or commanded to commit suicide for the most trivial of reasons.

Among other victims of Nero's displeasure at this time were Gaius Cassius Longinus and Lucius Junius Silanus Torquatus, the man originally betrothed to Nero's first wife Octavia. Lucius Antistius Vetus died together with his mother-in-law and daughter, as he was the father-in-law of Rubellius Plautus who had died in Asia. There were more deaths, among them Gallio and Annaeus Mela (Seneca's brothers), Rufrius Crispinus (in exile in Sar-

TIRIDATES

In 66 CE, a great celebration was held in Rome to mark the arrival of Tiridates, the newly approved king of Armenia. Tiridates's position had been confirmed by Roman general Corbulo after a series of campaigns and diplomatic discussions on the Eastern frontier. Tiridates was the brother of Parthian king Vologeses. He had, in fact, taken the throne of Armenia by agreement with his brother, which was contrary to how the Romans normally operated. But this had been approved by Corbulo on the condition that Tiridates came in person to Rome to show his allegiance to Nero. He worshiped the emperor as his god and the gates of the Temple of Janus were closed as a sign that the Roman world was now at peace. This visit was exceptionally lavish and expensive. According to tradition, Tiridates had 3,000 followers with him from Parthia, who were looked after at huge expense for nine months, the duration of their trip to and from Rome.

There was a public coronation for the new king in the Forum and the whole city was decorated to mark the occasion. Nero set a diadem on the king's head. Nero played the kithara and drove a chariot publicly, which apparently disgusted Tiridates. However, the Eastern ruler had the sense to keep quiet about his feelings, opting instead to flatter Nero on his achievements. Privately, he had much more respect for General Corbulo than for the emperor, but he kept his opinions to himself. In return, he managed to secure gifts of great value and riches needed to rebuild his capital city, Artaxata, which he also agreed to rename Neronia.

dinia), and the writer Petronius, who served as the emperor's advisor on good taste. Before his death, Petronius first ensured that his collection of valuable Greek vases was smashed to pieces, as he knew Nero had desired them. Tacitus described the series of killings as "a torrent of wasted bloodshed far from the battle line of active service, which depresses the mind." Yet nothing seemed to be able to hold Nero back, and Suetonius said that no moderation prevented Nero from murdering anyone he pleased.

In 66 CE, a senator of known integrity, Thrasea Paetus, was condemned to death by the Senate. It was quite clear that Nero would no longer tolerate dissension within the Senate, as Paetus had for several years withheld himself from the kind of flattery and ego massaging that the other senators had fallen into as a matter of course. His son-in-law, Helvidius Priscus, was condemned to exile at the same time.

It was in September of 66 CE that Nero decided to leave Rome and embark upon a tour of Greece. Until then he had not traveled abroad, but he had often complained that his skills could only be properly understood by Greek audiences. Until then Nero's favorite place of performance in Italy had been the theater at Neapolis, or Naples, a city founded by the Greeks. He wanted to perform in the country where he felt he would be best appreciated, so he made his plans to go on tour and visit many of the main cultural centers of Greece. On his way, he collected a great number of works of art as plunder from the treasuries and temples he visited.

It is difficult for us to appreciate why Nero had a fixation with performing and how he could justify to himself what came next. Traditionally, theatrical shows and athletic events in Greece had always been put on as contests, invariably of a religious nature. Almost all of the great Greek plays were written and acted out as competition entries. The festivals at Corinth, Delphi, and Olympia had been venues for sportsmen and performers, events held at intervals of four years or so, where participants came from all around the Greek world to compete against their fellow performers. Nero

Nero so loved performing that around 66 CE he headed to Greece where he felt his talents would be most appreciated.

decided to use his own absolute power to turn the system on its head. He left a freedman, Helius, in charge of events in Rome and took his guard prefect, Tigellinus, with him as well as the Augustans, who competed with him in the Greek games and plays. His wife, Statilia Messallina, also came as one of the party.

As Nero sailed to mainland Greece, a festival was held on Corcyra, the modern island of Corfu, and another at Actium, where the first emperor Augustus had once held games to celebrate his victory in a great battle against Mark Antony. Then Nero celebrated the so-called Isthmian Games at Corinth, where he announced the liberation of Greece. No more taxes would have to be paid to Rome, he said, and the country would have self-rule again. He then spent the winter in Greece, visiting more of the well-known centers of the arts, although it was said that he did not go to either Athens or Sparta. These two towns had been the most important centers in the country's history. Nero also did not take part in the Eleusinian Mysteries, a well-known event held near Athens. The reason for this may have been an embarrassing proclamation by the master of ceremonies that called for all criminals to stay away from the celebration. Since Nero had killed his mother, he should not have been allowed to attend. In the following year, 67 CE, all the main festivals were held in Greece, including a repeat of the Isthmian Games, as well as the Pythian Games at Delphi and the Olympic Games.

Nero played many parts in the Greek games and festivals, including acting in comedies and tragedies, playing the kithara, singing, and driving chariots. Even at the Olympic Games, where he fell out of his chariot and had to be helped back in again, he won first prize. In fact, everywhere he competed he was awarded the first prize, though we are told that he was always a nervous performer. It is very difficult to understand how a performer and competitor could take himself seriously knowing the outcome was so outrageously fixed, but Nero's megalomania was such that this indeed proved the case. He even contrived to hold new events at the games, such as a kithara-playing event at Olympia—which, of course, he won.

Toward the end of 67 CE, Nero came to Corinth, where he held a ceremony in which he took up a golden spade and cut the first trench in the ground for a new project, a canal across the

Isthmus of Corinth. He announced that this would benefit the people of Rome and himself, but conspicuously he did not mention the Senate in this, since by now he had come to disregard them in many ways.

Nero proposed the Corinth Canal, which would cut across the neck of the land (about 4 miles, or 6 kilometers across) and join mainland Greece's northernmost areas to a peninsula located to the south, known as the Peloponnese. The canal would enable much simpler transport of goods and people around the country. Unfortunately, the project came to an abrupt halt. The Corinth Canal would not be completed until 1893, many centuries after Nero began the project.

Nero began construction on the Corinth Canal toward the end of 67 CE, but it would not be completed until centuries later.

CHAPTER 5

AN EMPEROR'S DRAMATIC EXIT

While Nero was staying in Greece, two brothers, Rufus and Proculus Sulpicius Scribonius, governors of Upper and Lower Germany, got a nasty surprise when Nero summoned them. Although they had served Rome for many years, Nero now considered them a hazard to his throne. He forced them to commit suicide by slicing open their own veins. Nero's treachery did not stop there. In fact, some feel it got worse. General Cnaeus Domitius Corbulo had triumphed repeatedly for Rome along the Eastern frontier, but Nero sentenced him to death. Before Nero could act on his sentence, Corbulo used his own dagger to kill himself.

Nero may have forgotten the basis of his power, for the deaths of three such prominent generals was the signal for the army to begin

Leaders of Rome's army were usually members of the upper classes. They eventually began to object to Nero's actions and no longer supported him.

questioning what was happening. It has been said that Nero managed to hold onto the support of the ordinary Romans for much of his reign and that it was the upper classes, the senators and nobles of Rome, who grew to resent his abuse of power so much. It is a fact that most army leaders were chosen from these upper classes. With the generals so shamefully removed, the upper classes began to question their ongoing acceptance of Nero and of what he was doing to Rome. Nero's reign had been a time of relative peace and calm in the empire, so there was no need for soldiers to feel under threat. Yet it was probably the very absence of military activity that indicated a lack of interest on Nero's part, and now some commanders in the army began to question their future. Their loyalty to him could be abandoned, as they saw it, because he had not been loyal to them, a prerequisite for successful empire building. They could see little chance of improvement or security until Nero was removed from office.

ROMAN REBELLION

Toward the end of 67 CE, the storm clouds over Nero's reign began to gather. The freedman Helius, who, much to the disgust of the Senate had been left in control of affairs in Rome, came in person to Greece to fetch back the emperor. A famine was affecting the city because of a lack of grain ships arriving from Egypt, and there had also been an outbreak of disease in Rome. The people were already disaffected, and grew even more so when they saw cargoes of sand arriving in Rome from Alexandria to dress the arena where the imperial wrestlers would perform. Helius was worried that the news of Nero's dalliance in Greece would make them even angrier, so he urged him to return, which the emperor did in typical style. He came first to Naples, where he celebrated his many Greek victories, and then returned to Rome, ordering a section of the city wall to be pulled down so he could enter, as was done typically for victors of the Olympic Games. He climbed to the Temple of Apollo on the Palatine Hill and dedicated 1,808 crowns that he had won in various events. The scale and exaggeration of his successes must have repelled many onlookers, though it must have been an extraordinary spectacle.

By this time Nero had little or no interest at all in government. He continued to celebrate his achievements in Greece and continued to practice his performances. By March of 68 CE he was back in Naples, when news reached him of a revolt that had sprung up in Gallia Lugdunensis in the south of France. This was led by a Gaul named Caius Julius Vindex, whose last name meant "the avenger." Vindex had appealed to Servius Sulpicius Galba, general of Hispania Tarraconensis (Nearer Spain) for support and called for freedom from the tyrant. It seems likely that Vindex sought some kind of independence for Gaul as well as an end to Nero's rule, but Galba set his sights on becoming the next emperor. Vindex was blocked for some time by the new governor of Upper Germany, Verginius Rufus, but the revolution was under way and would prove impossible to stop. Vindex eventually committed suicide, probably in regret after seeing so many of his own people die. Verginius Rufus was urged by his soldiers to aim for the top job, but he refused to stand as a contender.

On April 2, 68 CE, Galba named himself legate of the Senate and people of Rome, notably not including emperor in his title. His claim to the throne had come into the open and the challenge was there to be met. He was supported by Nero's old friend Marcus Salvius Otho, governor of Lusitania in western Spain. When Nero heard this, he fainted.

Marcus Salvius Otho.

Afterward, he seemed more interested in discussing the merits of a new water organ that had been brought to him. The reaction of the Senate, humiliated for so long by Nero, was to condemn Galba as a public enemy but also to hold discussions with him about his actions. The fact was that Galba offered them a real opportunity to emerge from the tyranny of Nero, backed as he was by the Western armies. Nero's support began to crumble and his helpers started to disappear. Tigellinus, Nero's guard prefect, simply vanished and was replaced by Nymphidius Sabinus, whose relations with the Senate were good. This was a bad sign for Nero.

DESPERATE DESPOT

The emperor began to realize that he was beset by real problems, but failed to combat them in any meaningful way. If he had taken action by leading his armies to the west, where the rebellion had its epicenter, he may well have been able to rally considerable support from soldiers who had been loyal to his family since the time of Augustus. But as it was, his apparent cowardice took over. He asked his mistress, Calvia Crispinilla, to go to Africa to raise support, but this failed to materialize. He also summoned to Gaul the governor of Britain, Petronius Turpilianus. Nero did this to oppose the uprising, but this too had little effect, as Petronius became a supporter of Galba himself.

The historian Suetonius wrote that Nero dismissed the consuls and became sole consul himself in order to take control of events. He fell subject to deranged fantasies and thought of murdering all the senators, burning Rome, and escaping to Alexandria. When he spoke of his plans, the Senate finally acted, calling him a public enemy and stating their support for Galba, who had decided to march against Rome and take power by force. Nero suggested that if he went to Gaul and cried, standing unarmed before the battle line, the soldiers would take pity on him and relent. He considered writing songs of victory that would then be sung. The madness in him was complete, it seems, though he did decide not to make a speech in appeal to the people, for fear of being torn apart before reaching the Forum.

On June 8, 68 CE, Nero saw that his own praetorian guards were in rebellion, too. Their new prefect, Nymphidius Sabinus, had promised to support Galba; Sabinus paid his men 30,000 sesterces each to secure their agreement. The praetorian guards now declared Nero a public enemy—the final blow to Nero's power base. Nero disguised himself in an old cloak and hat and escaped from Rome to the villa of his freedman Phaon four miles (six kilometers) away.

Here, helped by his freedman Epaphroditus and attended by Acte, the freedwoman who had remained loyal to him throughout, Nero may have

Stories vary about how Nero died. He may have stabbed himself or he may have ordered someone else to do it for him.

stabbed himself in the throat with his sword. Other sources say that he ordered one of his subjects to do the dirty deed.

Even wounded and on the brink of death, Nero joked, “What loyalty, but you are too late!” as a centurion burst in with the intent to arrest or maybe even kill him. But he found the injured leader lay sprawled on the floor. The last words Nero uttered were “What an artist, I die!” Together with the nurses Ecloge and Alexandra, Acte buried his body. The thirty-year-old ruler was buried in Rome’s Domitii at the Campus Martius, the family tomb.

CHAPTER 6

REMEMBERING NERO

To get a balanced view of the events of Nero's life, we must try to see for ourselves exactly how evil Nero was, to what degree his name may have been disparaged unfairly, and indeed, how he was viewed in Rome after his death.

NERO'S EMPIRE

In terms of the larger empire, Nero had shown limited interest in government; little had been done during his reign to expand or consolidate Roman rule abroad.

There had been major unrest in Britain in 60 CE, when the revolt of Boudicca had wiped out around 70,000 inhabitants of Colchester, London, and St. Albans. Boudicca was queen of a tribe called the Iceni. When her husband Prasutagus died, the Romans refused to acknowledge her authority. Boudicca's daughters were raped and she was assaulted, precipitating her terrible revenge. Her revolt threatened to cause the Romans to abandon the province of Britain entirely. However, Governor Suetonius Paulinus put down the rebellion. Boudicca died, and stability in the province was restored. At this stage, the drive was to extend Roman control northward, beyond the legionary bases at Exeter, Lincoln, and the many other encampments that were spread out around the province. Plans to do this matured gradually, and within the next twenty years or so, three major new bases for the legions were built at Caerleon, Chester, and York. It should be observed, though, that this was not so much Nero's own policy as the continuation of what Claudius had first started in 43 CE.

On the Eastern frontier, problems with the Parthians had been ongoing for many years, but especially since 55 CE, when rival challenges for the Armenian throne arose in the north. This was very much at the edge of the Roman world and the Parthians were an unpredictable force. Their king, Vologeses, had appointed his brother Tiridates as the king of Armenia, as previously described. But

After a vicious assault on her daughters as well as herself, the Iceni queen Boudicca's revenge on the Romans was fierce.

Nero had refused to accept this and later appointed another man, Tigranes, in his place. Various cities were captured and then recaptured, including Volandum and Artaxata, which were destroyed by Romans under the command of Corbulo. Nero was hailed as imperator and a triumph was held in Rome in 58 CE to celebrate a great victory. However, this was a hollow claim, and the problems in Armenia were far from solved.

Eventually war broke out between Tigranes and Tiridates, while the Romans sided first with one and then the other. There was even disagreement between Corbulo and Lucius Caesennius Paetus, governor of Syria who had been sent by Nero to help. This resulted in Paetus being defeated by Tiridates and his men, while Corbulo came in afterward to pick up the pieces. The eventual outcome was that Tiridates publicly took off his crown and laid it before a statue of Nero in the field, agreeing to come to Rome and receive it back from the emperor in person. The history of the Armenian campaign is rather messy and won the emperor little glory, though he was again acclaimed as imperator on the arrival of Tiridates in Rome.

Tacitus is one of the three major sources about Nero's life, but all three portray the ruler in an extremely negative light.

The only other area of major conflict under Nero's reign was in Judea, modern-day Israel, where rebellion had broken out in 66 CE and was dealt with by the capable future emperor Vespasian. This was an extremely serious situation that led in turn to the sack of Jerusalem in 70 CE by Titus, Vespasian's son, and to the dismantling of the Hebrew kingdom. Toward the end of his reign, the situation was threatening and unclear as the Roman forces attempted to deal with the situation.

MISGUIDED ENTHUSIASM

One thing that certainly comes across in all accounts is Nero's tremendous enthusiasm, though it was so often misguided. His all-consuming passion for the theater and performance sets him apart from all other emperors and members of his social class, and it is referred to repeatedly by historians of the Roman period. Dio Cassius mentions a speech made by Julius Vindex during the revolt in Gaul, where he says that Nero disgraced the names of Caesar and Augustus through his acting and passion for theater. In order to understand how repellent this was at the time, one must understand that Nero used his position as emperor to secure a place on the stage and compel an audience of the Roman nobility to offer their applause.

Additionally, during that time, being an actor was not regarded as a fit occupation for an emperor or any upper-class Roman citizen. In this, Nero's self-degradation was obvious to all who witnessed his antics.

Nero's great love for participation in sport led him to coerce many of his countrymen, the Augustans in particular, to take part in games such as the Neronia in 60 and 65 CE. Suetonius writes that Nero compelled 400 senators and 600 nobles to do battle in the amphitheater. It is hard to imagine that these people all participated willingly, even if the numbers have been exaggerated. During Nero's trip to Greece, he took a large number of followers with him, including the Augustans, whose job must have been to compete in events against Nero. The sheer number of prizes he won—1,808 in total—shows how much their role was merely a token, or a support mechanism for massaging one man's ego. Effectively, their job was to lose or be runners-up to their boss. In this, we see how misguided his enthusiasm to perform was, as it led him to humiliate so many of those who should have been his genuine supporters.

OTHER ISSUES

The historians also state that the promotion of freedmen to senior positions led to discontent, such

THE AFTERMATH

After Nero's death, the Roman world experienced major political turmoil and was turned on its head for at least twelve months while four men vied for supreme control. Each of the four men—Galba, Otho, Vitellius, and Vespasian—became, in turn, the emperor of Rome, supported and brought to power by their own military factions. Nero's legacy (as the last of the Julian line) was to see the transfer of power change from being a dynastic, family-driven process to a competitive system where the most powerful army general would have the best chance of success. It is true that can see him falling off his chariot at Olympia and still not really caring, safe in the knowledge that he would win the race anyway. When Lucius Caesennius Paetus returned to Rome from his failed campaign in Armenia, he is said to have been terrified of what Nero might do to him. But Nero actually let him off, saying that he thought it was unfair to keep such a timid man in suspense as to what might happen to him. Nero was bound to be rejected by the senators and nobles whom he had for so long humiliated. Yet none of this lessens our interest in hearing more about him or our fascination with all the other things he might have said or done. After Nero's death, the Roman world experienced major political turmoil and was turned on its head for at least twelve months while four men vied for supreme control. Each of the four men—Galba, Otho, Vitellius, and Vespasian—became, in turn, the emperor of Rome, supported and brought to power by their own military factions. Nero's legacy (as the last of the Julian line) was to see the transfer of power change from being a dynastic, family-driven process to a competitive system where the most powerful army general would have the best chance of success. It is true that once Vespasian took over a new dynasty was begun, that of the Flavians, and that gradually stability returned to Rome. It seemed for a while that the old days were back when the empire could be inherited, but in reality this proved short-lived.

There were many left after his death who did mourn Nero genuinely, however. In looking at portraits of the emperor, it is possible to see him like we see rock stars today, an Elvis Presley figure perhaps, with a curling lip and a strangely captivating smile who after his death was regularly "seen" by people all over the world. Nero imitators who sang to the accompaniment of the kithara turned up in different parts of the empire, as if the Romans could not accept that their larger-than-life emperor had actually died.

as when Anicetus was put in charge of the fleet at Misenum and Helius was left in charge of affairs in Rome during the emperor's time in Greece. Helius was accused of abusing his position by Dio Cassius as he was apparently guilty of putting to death Sulpicius Camerinus, a leading senator. This must have been hard to accept for those who saw the freedman as a social inferior brought to prominence on the whim of the emperor. Nero's predecessor, Claudius, had also been accused many times of giving away excessive authority to his private staff of freedmen, and this brought him into disrepute with many of the senators. Nero had sworn on his accession not to fall into the same habits, but it became clear that he made this promise without any sincerity.

Other promises made at the beginning of Nero's rule included one that he would not, as Claudius had done so often, hold trials behind closed doors. But toward the end of his reign, it appears that Nero's system of justice was entirely arbitrary. So many deaths are mentioned in all the sources that we cannot assume them all to be lies. Nero clearly removed anyone he perceived to stand in his way without compunction or real reason.

Tacitus says that Pallas, the ex-freedman of Claudius, was killed for being too rich, and Suetonius says that Thrasea Paetus's flaw was looking like a grumpy old schoolmaster. In fact, Nero was always jealous of anyone else who caught public attention. This seems to have been a crime that only the bold around him would dare commit. In the same way, when the emperor did confer liberty to his subjects, it was seen as a gift conferred by an all-powerful ruler, not a right. By these tokens, we can see that the resentment building up against Nero was quite real and justified. Nero's private life has been variously described by historians, but all seem to agree that he had multiple marriages to women and to men, some of whom seem to have been chosen deliberately for their strange habits. He seems to have publicly acted out his sexual perversions, and Suetonius mentions that he forced the wives of Roman noblemen to act as prostitutes in temporary brothels, serving not only his own needs but those of anyone else. This took place during a barge trip from Rome to Ostia and, if true, can only have aggravated the bad feelings growing toward Nero among the senators and nobles. Even if exaggerated, this story shows how Nero was viewed shortly

An illustration of a bust of Emperor Nero signed by P. Sellier.

after his death. If the story had not been believable, it would probably not have been included. Another story passed on by Suetonius says that Nero raped a vestal virgin called Rubria. This is not mentioned by the other two writers and could well be untrue, like many accounts in modern-day tabloid newspapers. However, if we consider that the modern-day equivalent of a vestal virgin would be a nun, the act described would have been truly horrific.

Suetonius refers to Nero's dreadful treatment of the Senate, mentioning how he sometimes seized the estates of those who had died but had not left enough of their possessions to him as emperor. Suetonius also claims that when appointing magistrates, Nero said, "You know what I need. Let's see that nobody else is left with anything." The constant plundering of property was needed to pay for all the excesses that went with Nero's reign, and for the first time since Augustus became emperor, money was always in short supply. Again, the impact of this must have been considerable, as upper-class Romans saw the state coffers become depleted through one man's lust and greed.

One of the most horrific crimes committed

by Nero was that of matricide, the murder of his mother, Agrippina. In an ordinary Roman's eyes, family unity was very important, and a man's mother was to be honored.

The repeated mention of incest between the emperor and his mother is a reminder of how degraded the relationship was considered to be at the time, and the calculated plotting of her death shows Nero in a terrible light. Tacitus mentions that at Nero's birth, a fortuneteller had predicted that he would kill his mother and become emperor, but Agrippina had said, "Let him kill me, provided that he becomes emperor." There seems to be little doubt that not only did he actually did kill her, but he enjoyed doing so.

Nero's crimes included a program of persecutions against the Christians, which started sometime after the great fire in 64 CE. Nero may have had his reasons for setting this train of events into motion, but his excessive cruelty must have offended many who witnessed it, Christian and non-Christian. The new faith had recently spread from the province of Judea (modern-day Israel) and was beginning to make an impact on Rome itself, where several of its guiding principles clashed strongly with the

History is teeming with accounts of Nero's crimes and atrocities, yet he is often portrayed as a fanciful figure.

accepted state religion. The group of established Roman gods was headed by Jupiter Optimus Maximus, or Jupiter the Greatest and Best, whose control of divine forces was mirrored in human terms by the emperor's control of his people. Christianity threatened this system. Its followers maintained that since there was only one god, Jupiter and his fellow gods did not exist. This belief was supported by the beliefs of another non-Christian sect from Judea that the Romans sometimes confused with the Christians. These were the Jews, who believed that there was only one god and that they were his chosen people. While the normally adaptable Romans would accept new gods into their system and remain perfectly happy about it, these two new religious groups from Judea both had faiths that made it impossible for Romans to accept them. Nero was in some sense really reacting against a religion that threatened the very fabric of Roman society. His persecution of Christians has to be seen in this light to be fully understood, though it certainly does not justify his reaction. Nero's reputation with future generations was greatly colored by this affair. The European tradition that has blackened his name and portrayed him as an evil monster is a Christian tradition. It is perhaps his assault on the Christians and his responsibility for the deaths of Peter and Paul, in particular, that have caused him to remain a hated figure throughout history.

Strange though it seems, however, Nero is often written about by historians as a whimsical figure. His sense of humor combined with his passion for all kinds of performance endears him to the reader and gives him a kind of charm, though this may be hard to accept given his brutality and horrendous behavior. One cannot help but see him as a larger-than-life, misguided bundle of energy and enthusiasm, who even made jokes at his own death. We can see him falling off his chariot at Olympia and still not really caring, safe in the knowledge that he would win the race anyway. When Lucius Caesennius Paetus returned to Rome from his failed campaign in Armenia, he is said to have been terrified of what Nero might do to him. But Nero actually let him off, saying that he thought it was unfair to keep such a timid man in suspense as to what might happen to him. Nero was bound to be rejected by the senators and nobles whom he had for so long humiliated. Yet none of this lessens our interest in hearing more about him or our fascination with all the other things he might have said or done.

MOVING ON

Immediately after the death of Nero, Servius Sulpicius Galba became the next emperor of Rome, until his death in early 69 CE. He did not realize that the extent of his power was due to the praetorian guards. He failed to pay them properly, so they turned against him and killed him.

Marcus Salvius Otho became emperor of Rome after causing a rebellion and deposing Galba. He was defeated by the forces of Vitellius and committed suicide in April of 69 CE. Tigellinus disappeared as guard prefect in early 68 CE and was officially replaced by a colleague, Nymphidius Sabinus. Sabinus was forced to commit suicide during the rule of Otho in early 69 CE. Tiridates was removed from power as king of Armenia in 72 CE, when a tribe called the Alans marched against his kingdom. He was not mentioned again in historical sources.

Titus Flavius Vespasianus (Vespasian) raised a

Servius Sulpicius Galba.

rival claim to the throne against Vitellius in July 69 CE. He caused Vitellius's downfall and established a new dynasty, the Flavians, as rulers of Rome. After his death in 79 CE, his sons Titus and Domitian became the next emperors.

Nero's mythology lived on for many years after his death, finding its way into literature and popular folklore alike. Such is the legacy of Nero, whose story will always be available to fascinate us.

centurion A leader of one hundred men in the ancient Roman Army, known as a century.

colonia A Roman town or settlement where all the inhabitants had the status of full Roman citizens.

consul The title given to one or two very senior Roman magistrates, men who had reached the top of the *cursus honorum*. It is the equivalent to a modern-day prime minister or president, though a consul was still subject to the emperor. The emperor sometimes served as consul himself.

consul designate Someone who was selected for the job of consul in an upcoming year.

dais A kind of throne or other seat or platform that signified respect.

despot A leader who is usually harsh or unfair and holds absolute power.

diadem A crown or other type of headband often decorated with jewels, which is worn to show power.

Forum Romanum The Forum was the center of Rome. It consisted of many public buildings, including temples, shops, and law courts.

freedman A person who once had been a slave but was later released. Freedmen often continued to maintain a social and business relationship with their former masters and, in particular, freedmen were often employed as trusted individuals by the emperors.

imperator This title was given to a general who had been victorious in battle. It was often used as a term to indicate the emperor himself, but had its origins in military life.

kithara An instrument similar to a guitar (the word "guitar" in fact derives from kithara), having strings and played to accompany someone singing. It is also often referred to as a lyre or a harp.

legate In ancient Rome, a general or governor of a region; also can refer to his deputy.

megalomania A fixation with using authority, usually including controlling others; an illusion of one's power or importance.

plebeian This term was given to a member of the plebs, the ordinary people of Rome. It is used to distinguish lower-class citizens from the rest of society.

praetorian Having the powers of the praetor, who was one of two judges in ancient Rome whose rank was just under that of the consul.

republic This term is often used for the Roman state, represented by the acronym SPQR, meaning the Senate and People of Rome. After Augustus became the first emperor of Rome, the republic was, in effect, an empire controlled by one man, but the illusion was maintained carefully that the republic still existed and that the Senate and people were as important as they had always been in Rome's early history.

Senate A body of about 600 senior statesmen whose authority combined with the emperor's. The Senate acted as the lawgiving body of Rome; its importance in Roman history cannot be overestimated.

sesterce A type of coin in ancient Rome, which was the same amount as one-quarter of a denarius.

toga A woolen garment worn by Romans. A ceremony took place when a boy put on a man's toga for the first time, usually around the age of fourteen. It was a big event in a young person's life.

FOR MORE INFORMATION

American Classical League
860 NW Washington Boulevard, Suite A
Hamilton, OH 45013
(513) 529-7741
Website: https://www.aclclassics.org
The American Classical League was founded to foster the study of classical languages in the United States and Canada.

Department of Classics
P.O. Box 117435
University of Florida
Gainesville, FL 32611-7435
Email: schmelin@ufl.edu
Website: http://www.ancientnarrative.com/
The articles in the Ancient Narrative journal focus on Greek, Roman, and Jewish novelistic traditions.

Archaeological Institute of America Headquarters
Boston University
656 Beacon Street, 6th Floor
Boston, MA 02215-2006
Email: aia@aia.bu.edu
Website: https://www.archaeological.org
The Archaeological Institute of America (AIA) is the oldest and largest group in North America that dedicates itself to all things archaeology.

California Classical Association—Northern Section
Attn: Gillian McIntosh, Treasurer
581 Frederick Street
San Francisco, CA 94117
Website: http://www.ccanorth.org/

The CCA encourages the instruction and training of the classics, such as through conferences and relationships with other classical organizations.

National Junior Classical League
860 NW Washington Blvd, Suite A
Hamilton, OH 45013
(513) 529-7741
Email: info@njcl.org
Website: http://www.njcl.org

This division of the American Classical League was formed in 1936 for junior and senior high school students. It seeks to inspire a curiosity in and an appreciation of ancient Roman and Greek language, literature, and culture, with a focus on understanding its effects on modern culture.

Society for Classical Studies (SCS)
University of Pennsylvania220 S. 40th Street
Suite 201E
Philadelphia, PA 19104-3512
(215) 898-4975
E-mail: info@classicalstudies.org

Website: https://classicalstudies.org/
Founded as the American Philological Association, the SCS is North America's foremost society for the study of the languages, literatures, and civilizations of ancient Rome and Greece.

WEBSITES

Because of the changing nature of internet links, Rosen Publishing has developed an online list of websites related to the subject of this book. This site is updated regularly. Please use this link to access the list:

http://www.rosenlinks.com/LANW/nero

Allan, Tony. *Exploring the Life, Myth, and Art of Ancient Rome* (Civilizations of the World). New York, NY: Rosen Publishing, 2012.

Bard, Mary. *SPQR: A History of Ancient Rome.* New York, NY: Liveright Publishing, 2015.

Benoit, Peter. *Ancient Rome* (The Ancient World). New York, NY: Children's Press, 2013.

Bingham, Jane. *Classical Myth: A Treasury of Greek and Roman Legends, Art, and History* (World of Mythology) Armonk, NY: M.E. Sharpe, 2014.

Brandon, S. G. F. *Beliefs, Rituals, and Symbols of Ancient Greece and Rome* (Man, Myth & Magic). New York, NY: Cavendish Square Publishing, 2014.

Campbell, Duncan B. *The Rise of Imperial Rome, AD 14–193*. Oxford, UK: Osprey Publishing, 2013.

Heather, P.J. *The Fall of the Roman Empire: A New History of Rome and the Barbarians.* New York, NY: Oxford University Press, 2010.

Knox, Peter E., and J. C. McKeown. *The Oxford Anthology of Roman Literature.* New York, NY: Oxford University Press, 2013.

Kuiper, Kathleen. *Ancient Rome: From Romulus and Remus to the Visigoth Invasion* (Britannica Guide to Ancient Civilizations). New York, NY: Britannica Educational Publishing, 2011.

Marshall Cavendish. *Ancient Rome: An Illustrated History*. New York, NY: Marshall Cavendish Reference, 2012. EBook.

Benario, Herbert W. "Nero (54–68 A.D.)" *De Imperatoribus Romanis*: An Online Encyclopedia of Roman Rulers and Their Families. November 10, 2006. Retrieved April 26, 2016 (http://www.roman-emperors.org/nero.htm).

Bishop, John. *Nero: The Man and the Legend.* New York, NY: A. S. Barnes, 1965.

Claridge, Amanda. *Rome*. Oxford, England: Oxford University Press, 1998.

Cook, S. A., et al. *The Cambridge Ancient History, Volume X*. Cambridge, England: Cambridge University Press, 1966.

Dio Cassius. *Roman History, Books 61 to 70.* Cambridge, England: Loeb Classical Library, 2000.

Draper, Robert. "Rethinking Nero." *National Geographic*. September 2014. Retrieved April 25, 2016 (http://ngm.nationalgeographic.com/2014/09/emperor-nero/draper-text).

Franzero, Charles Marie. *The Life and Times of Nero.* London: A. Redman, 1954.

Grant, Michael. *Nero*. London: Weidenfeld & Nicolson, 1970.

Griffin, Miriam T. *Nero: The End of a Dynasty*. London, England: Batsford, 1984.

"Nero." PBS. 2006. Retrieved April 25, 2016 (http://www.pbs.org/empires/romans/empire/nero.html).

Scullard, Hugh H. *From the Gracchi to Nero*. London, England: Methuen, 1959.

Suetonius. *The Twelve Caesars*. London: Penguin, 1957.

Tacitus. *The Annals of Imperial Rome*. London: Penguin, 1956.

Wasson, Donald L. "Nero." Ancient History Encyclopedia. June 29, 2012. Retrieved April 26, 2016 (http://www.ancient.eu/Nero/).

D

E

F

G

H

I

J

K

L

M

ABOUT THE AUTHORS

Zoe Lowery is an avid student of history, constantly reading and getting lost in the fascinating stories like that of Nero. She has written and edited a number of history books for Rosen Publishing, Gareth Stevens Publishing, Enslow Publishing, and PowerKids Press. She enjoys a quiet afternoon in the library. She lives in Colorado.

Julian Morgan earned his B.A. in Greek studies at Bristol University, England, in 1979. He also earned a master's degree in computers and education at King's College, London, in 1990. He has been head of classics at Derby Grammar School. Julian has a special interest in software design and has published many programs, including ROMANA and Rome the Eternal City, through his business, J-PROGS. He is a member of the American Classical League's Committee on Educational Computer Applications. He is the computing coordinator for the Joint Association of Classical Teaching (JACT) and has a regular column, "Computanda," in their bulletin. He also runs a training business called Medusa, which specializes in helping teachers of classics to use information technology in their teaching.

PHOTO CREDITS

Cover, pp. 3, 32–33 DEA/G. Dagli Orti/De Agostini/Getty Images; cover (background) Bettmann/Getty Images; p. 7 Vatican Museums and Galleries, Vatican City/Alinari/Bridgeman Images; p. 13 © Peter Horree/Alamy Stock Photo; p. 14 DEA/A. De Gregorio/De Agostini/Getty Images; pp. 18, 42 Werner Forman/Universal Images Group/Getty Images; pp. 21, 95 Alinari Archives/Getty Images; p. 24 © Konstantinos Tsakalidis/Alamy Stock Photo; p. 27 DEA Picture Library/Getty Images; pp. 28–29 Heritage Images/Hulton Fine Art Collection/Getty Images; p. 35 DEA/Archivio J. Lange/De Agostini/Getty Images; pp. 36–37 © The Print Collector/Alamy Stock Photo; p. 39 Giorgio Cosulich/Getty Images; p. 43 © Ferdinando Piezzi/Alamy Stock Photo; p. 46 Kean Collection/Archive Photos/Getty Images; pp. 48–49 DEA/P. De Antonis/De Agostini/Getty Images; pp. 52–53, 81 Time Life Pictures/The LIFE Picture Collection/Getty Images; pp. 56–57 Universal History Archive/Universal Images Group/Getty Images; p. 63 LL/Roger Viollet/Getty Images; p. 66 lexan/iStock/Thinkstock; p. 68, 72, 75 Hulton Archive/Getty Images; p. 79 Print Collector/Hulton Archive/Getty Images; p. 88 Stock Montage/Archive Photos/Getty Images; p. 91 Universal Images Group/Getty Images; interior pages background images © iStockphoto.com/kikkalek5050 (sky), Triff/Shutterstock.com (map).

Designer: Brian Garvey; Editor: Heather Moore Niver; Photo Researcher: Heather Moore Niver